This is my journal, my notes and my thoughts.

I am:

INTRODUCTION

Only you can change your life and you have to want to. Nobody can do it for you. Or you may be happy with your life would like something new to try and a new way to motivate yourself.

Being happy is something that is "in" you. Life will throw problems at you but it is how you deal with them that matters.

In a world of chaos and chattering voices, doubts, anxiety, depression and chemically induced worry due to additives and other influences sometimes you need to put your hand up and say "No more!" or at least "Time Out!".

In a world of *"Emotional Vampires"* (those who drain your energy by needing attention themselves) and those to gain their emotional strength by what they perceive as "Personal Power" at your expense (those who drain your self confidence while bolstering their own by "putting you down" needlessly) you would benefit from being able to recognize them for who they are and then they have no power at all! With the latter it can actually start making you stronger if you can start analysing what they are doing and saying and looking at what they are saying. Are you actually right? Are you actually doing things right? If the answer is "yes" then that then negates all their comments forever. Conversely they could be doing it out of fear that you are becoming confident and able to look after yourself. That is their insecurity, not yours!

There are many expensive things you can buy to help you. Many are pretty and lovely things which are a joy to own. Some people find benefit from them, some don't. They probably all work but I've found there are simpler ways and ways to help the world as well. Recycling and Affirmations is one way. There is a beauty in "things" you wouldn't normally "value" without giving them a value in themselves but giving them a use, a repurpose, then they have a greater value to you. They may have been created for one thing, but their future may lay in another.

Take for instance the Coffee Jar. A simple glass jar with a lid. It holds the granules that go into the cup. It isn't just a cup of coffee though, it has purpose.

If caffeinated then that cup could be a wake up, energy but also a certain amount of anxiety and stress which caffeine itself causes. It could signify the start of your day and stepping from restful sleep to the challenges of the day. It could signify a break from work, that "breather" when you go to the coffee point and make your drink. It has a lot more meaning than "just" a cup of coffee (or tea!). Or it has no meaning at all, it is just a hot beverage. There are undoubtedly a few "stress factors" with coffee (and tea) but that may have to be a trade off if you have a lot to do and a pleasant addition to the day that is the reward and the "carrot" that gets you through the time to the next cup.

If decaffeinated then the taste and relaxation of the cup which is reassuringly there.

But, is it more? A cup of coffee (or tea) can be drunk alone or socially. It can be that cup that makes the difference because you are drinking it with friends. It can be the excuse to meet up. It can have meaning if it is the cup you discuss a problem over. That spoonful can be for so many different reasons. I'm specifically mentioning coffee because of the jar.

What of the jar? What is its destiny after all those spoonfuls are gone? Back to recycling? There more energy will melt it and repurpose it. Or, does it have a future with you?

What I'm trying to encourage here is seeing things as having a purpose after their original purpose is over but in a way that will support you emotionally, mentally and physically.

Everything that happens to you shapes you. Every word and deed you pass by, everything you see along the way is an experience. Likewise everything you say and do influences others. A kind word or a smile can change someone's day, however you may feel yourself. You never know, someone smiling at you might change your day for the better too.

Problems are challenges to be got over. Every one you deal with empowers you! By the time you read this you will have survived years of problems and solutions, congratulate yourself. They aren't trivial, they are all important as they have made you, you.

The road is long from birth to death. It has many twists and turns, many landmarks along the way. Everything you see, say or do is a part of you and it is your choice what you do with the experiences and what people say. Many pass "unmarked" but they are very important to you. This is what I'm attempting to address with some of the ideas in this book.

When someone utters words those words are theirs to speak. It is up to you how you receive those words. If they are worth listening to, listen and take them in. If they are self-serving for the person who spoke them then pity the speaker, understand them but put up a little emotional wall and say to yourself internally, those words aren't for me. Let them wash over you.

THE OLE GLASS JAR: Gift of Light

I thought I'd start with this one as we all have glass jars we have finished with. They stand there, empty and "unwanted" at the end of their original purpose, destined for the fires of recreation. Or, they can be destined for the "fire of your own re-creation".

Some jars are "prettier" than others. Some are just functional but they all have a re-use.

The obvious use is for jams, jellies and preserves.

The less obvious are for candles. Candles bring light, hope and warmth (physically and for the soul) so repurposing the jars and rescuing and remelting wax has a meaning in itself. You can take the wax, take the essential oils and other things and make a new candle. This will also provide light and love for those who share it or if you give it as a gift it has that additional element of the care you have shown in making something for someone. Each candle has had a past before. But, in the melting pot that past is irrelevant, its future is something else, something new. It may have been abandoned, part burnt, damaged and deemed useless or a gift from someone who couldn't use it but it will be a light in the darkness for someone else. If you ask in Charity

Shops sometimes they have candles they can't sell but would be happy to give to you. Wicks are readily available and instructions are available on the internet but the basics are put the wick in the jar, melt the wax carefully and pour it carefully in, leave it to cool and you have a candle.

Even going out to hunt for those candles is a positive action. Then when the candles have been sorted into colour and type of wax, so that there is a harmony in the making, they will then make something beautiful ready for their new life.

There is an irony in filling coffee jars with candles as the coffee itself may have brought people together and brought light from a conversation. The future of that jar is to bring more light and happiness in a safe way as the lid can be put on when the candle is blown out. Then the jar will be empty again... Or it can be an empty jar to start with... Empty or full of potential?

There is space in this book for you to write your ideas and thoughts if you cannot get to a piece of paper to put into a jar. You can always write them out again later, cut them up and put them in your jar.

You may wish to use this book as your Journal and a place to write. It is your book, your space, nobody can tell you what to do and if you want it that way nobody needs to ever read it. So you can write what you like and get those thoughts out of your head!

MINDFULNESS JARS

Take stock of your life? Too hard, too true! If you feel overwhelmed then perhaps a time to have a "Jar" in your life. They can be for many reasons. I've put a few ideas here.

HAPPY JAR

Exercise

Take a jar with a lid and a piece and paper and a pen. If you have the time then light a candle and put on some music that you really like, shut the door and keep everyone out. This is your time of calm and your time to think.

On that piece of paper write all the good things that have happened to you. One by one as you can remember them. Don't worry about "getting them all" or the order as once you have created your jar you can add to it at any time when you think of something.

Write them as a list, one below the other leaving a bit of space between them.

Then take a pair of scissors and cut them out so that they lay on the table in front of you, lots of slips of paper of all the happy times in your life. Then one by one pick them up, fold them up so the writing is on the inside, thank them and put them in the jar.

When there are dark times, as there always must be, take one of them out of the jar and remember that happy time.

The Happy Jar could cost you very little, but it could mean a lot!

If you have the time or ongoing as you find things during happy occasions you can decorate your Happy Jar. It may be that a necklace you love breaks and you can't fix it, so tie it to your Jar. That necklace has brought you happiness, it can then continue to do so. It may be your baby's hair ribbon that no longer has a "purpose" but it has meaning for you, tie it to the jar and you'll still have it and it can bring you a smile when you go to your jar.

If you feel lost, alone or in need of cheering up, reach into the jar and all those memories are there.

If you think of another memory, write it and fold it, thank it and put it in the jar.

Just seeing all those bits of paper may well help you to think of your life a bit differently.

If there aren't enough bits of paper in the jar go out and make some happy memories!

Exercise

*Take another jar, your piece of paper and a pen and write down all the things that **would** make you happy. Then go and do them. When you have done them put that slip of paper in the jar.*

You can always "catch up" even if you feel you haven't had enough happy memories.

Sometimes just giving yourself the time to think of the good will drive back that black wall of problems.

ACTION JAR

If you can't think of something to do because the world is chattering too much then it is time to stop and think. This means taking a breath and stopping for a moment.

"Stopping" doesn't mean shutting yourself in a room but obviously that would be the best way! If you are on the train or the bus, that is "your" time. The very nature of trains and busses means that people do not talk or "bother you". That is valuable time!

Exercise

1.   Keep a small plastic non-recyclable cup. Put a hole in the bottom. Find some soil. Find a plant (doesn't matter what it is, weeds are just plants out of place) and plant it. Take time every day to give that plant a little bit of water. That is your "happy time".

2.   Take a short walk and look for "Nature out of Place". It can be a piece of grass in the concrete, it can be a leaf which has blown from a tree. However much we create concrete boxes for ourselves nature will always win through. If you would like to take a photo, take a photo and keep that memory in your phone.

3.   *Feel the breeze on your face. When you are walking take a moment to feel the air touching you, the breeze. Watch it blowing your hair, or a leaf. The wind blows in towns and cities as much as it does in the countryside. That wind has always blown, it will blow long after you are gone. Then focus on that breeze blowing your troubles away. Throw your problems into the air and imagine them gone. Then think about how you can make them gone!*

4.   *Take a moment at home to turn everything off which makes noise and sit and enjoy the peace.*

When you get home, on the train or when you get a moment, write what you have thought and what you would like to do.

TAKE A HIKE

(THE MEMORY JAR)

That is exactly what you want your worries to do. They chitter, chatter and make things so much worse. There is no glory in them, let them go. They don't help and they won't solve anything. Only in the quiet moments when you can think will you think your way out of a problem and find solutions. It is oh so easy to focus on the problem and let it drag you down.

That won't get rid of it but it is a start on the journey to get rid of it.

Everyday life around you probably doesn't help. There are so many things you have to do and the more you worry about what hasn't been done the more this piles up both physically and emotionally. To be able to sort the problem you need clarity, time and space. It is up to you to make that space. By space I don't just mean physically, I mean a chance in your mind to think a situation through, to work out how to do "a job" or to find a solution to a problem.

Exercise

If you can then take a moment to plan a little trip. Just a short walk or something more complicated perhaps. There are places everywhere that you can do this. Plan your trip or be spontaneous. Make sure you have the right coat, the right boots as you don't want a distraction or it to be unpleasant. Make sure people you love and who are living with you know you are going. Then you can step out of that door without worrying.

Perhaps you can do it in a lunch hour at work. Make yourself a picnic and take it to the park or at least a bench somewhere. Anywhere that is away from your everyday workplace or home.

This is your time but it isn't just the walk, it is a chance to focus. On your walk choose something like a leaf or a flower. That one flower is the most important thing in the world.

Stand with both feet firmly on the ground and take a deep breath in then let it out slowly, breathing out all your worries. All that matters at that moment is what you are focusing on.

It is beautiful, it has taken many thousands of years for that one thing to be in that one place at this particular time. For that moment in time what you are seeing is perfect, the next moment it will be different but still perfect.

It is part of a cycle of life and part of all that there is. In that one moment in the world everything is as it is, the next moment it will be different as things change.

Same with problems. They are as they are now but it only takes a solution or being able to deal with them and life will move on.

When you walk on, watch the ground and see if you can find something, perhaps an acorn, a leaf, a stick and bring it back with you.

When you get back home find a jar that you don't need anymore. It can be any size and from anything, jam, mustard, coffee and that is your Memory Jar. It is the place where you keep your totally free treasures.

You probably won't remember which walk they were from and when you got them but as your jar gains its little collection of things you will know you had those walks and that is sometimes enough. They are a reminder of the time and space you had and how easy it is to make that escape. You are never trapped.

EXERCISE

Take a moment wherever you are (as long as it is safe to do so, not while driving please!) and sit down or stand still. Take a deep breath in and let it out slowly. Imagine you are in a beautiful woodland or beside the sea, or somewhere else you would like to be. Not a real place or a memory. This is "Your Place". It comes from your imagination and nobody else can be there or go there.

Look around you and commit it to memory. What is on the floor at your feet? Are there trees? Are there birds?

This is your space and your escape. When you feel the world is getting you down you can call up this image and remember the peace and tranquillity there is there. You can't change any situation but you can change how you deal with it and get that inner Serenity that allows you to deal with it.

In that place create a waterfall for yourself. The cool waters flow down over a shelf into a pool below.

Step into that water flow and feel the water flowing down over your head, your shoulders, your arms, down your body, down your legs, washing your worries with it, taking the stress with it.

Problems mount up if they aren't dealt with and sometimes you just can't deal with them, which makes more problems. Admitting that the situation has got the better of you is a start. Finding the space to be able to think clearly is the start of the solution.

When you get back from your walk you can start planning how you are going to solve your problems!

JARRING EVENT

There comes a time in everyone's life when there is a major life event. It can be good or bad but one thing is certain the memory will stay with you forever.

In time that memory will fade and in some ways if it is a bad event that is exactly what you want it to do.

Here it is best to have **a jar** and **a box**.

EXERCISE

For the jar write down, on bits of paper or piece of paper and cut it up later, all the happy bits of a memory which is troubling you. You could take a moment at any time and perhaps keep paper and pen with you, perhaps in your wallet or purse to write down thoughts when you get the chance. Or you can write your thoughts here if you carry this book with you.

In a digital age there are no longer photos you can hold and "feel the moment". Images flicker on the screen but that doesn't have the same physical grounding as a photograph may have. So, perhaps you'd like to keep paper which has been "misprints" and then print out small versions of your photographs and put them in your Jar to remember a specific event.

If there are physical things you can keep from that event e.g. a twig from the ground, a shell, a feather then put that in your jar as well. These things have no value monetarily but emotionally they are priceless because they are a part of that day.

If the event is an unpleasant one then write down those memories and put them into a cardboard box. Then burn the box somewhere that it is safe to burn it. As it burns let those memories go with it and accept that they are the past and you don't need them anymore.

Life is swirling around you and you are lost in the events that are happening all too fast but time progresses, tick tock, in a regular fashion. It may seem that things are flying by but that is just how things seem.

That Special Day Jar

Exercise

Take a moment, take a deep breath and take a piece of paper and write down your feelings, snippets of comments you want to remember and words that sum up the day and put them in a special jar when you get home. Look around for a stone, pebble or something like that. Something physical which is "from" that day.

When you have a quiet moment and the fun is over then take some time to put these things in a jar and decorate it or label it so that you have a jar from that day to remember when you may need it.

Feng Shui and clearing energy can be great but you are clearing away your happy memories too, focuses on times gone by and hope for happy times in the future.

When they are there they "hang" in your line of sight but also work on your subconscious to give you a contentment.

Family photographs and photos of happy days too. You can't do this so much with an electronic photo. You might flip past them on the way to something else but there is nothing like sitting there and having them "with you".

JARRING AFFIRMATIONS

When you feel doubt or need a bit of guidance or reassurance it could be time to turn to your Affirmations Jar.

This is something that only you can set up but it is easy and cheap to do, it just takes your time. I could list a whole lot of affirmations here for you to print out, cut up and put in your jar but they wouldn't be personal to you. These have to be YOUR affirmations. Please take a moment to write them here so that you can write them out later, cut them up and put them in your jar.

Today we have the Internet and there are plenty of photographs of sheets of Affirmations. It is a resource which is yours to use so why not type "Affirmations" into the search box and then take a look through what you find and write the ones that you like here.

When you have a quiet moment you can add to them, write them down on a sheet of paper, cut them out, fold them up and put them in your jar.

Idea

It may be amusing to take "Junk Mail" and cut out the non printed parts of it. You'll then have paper of various colours to write on which only have been

rubbish but could now be something important to you.

Write your Affirmations on these slips of paper, fold them up and put them in your jar (which was also free as you bought the contents and have already enjoyed that).

When you have a good selection take one piece of paper out a day, write what it says in your diary and try to focus on that all day and actually "do it".

HEART-FELT AFFIRMATIONS

Why not write your affirmations onto a heart? There are plenty of pictures of heart shapes on the internet for you to choose your favourite. Perhaps you would like to print a few out to write in or you could draw a heart freehand. Once you have cut a template you can cut as many as you like. Then you can write on them, fold them in half and put them in your jar.

If you want to make a more permanent Affirmation why not cut the heart from felt and embroider or write the affirmation on the heart and hang it in your room.

You could take a clothes hanger and some string and hang multiple hearts. If you need a specific Affirmation one day, take it down, put it in your bag or pocket and carry it with you.

JAR LIST

This is like a "Bucket List" but smaller scale.

There will be times in your life when you question "What have I done?". Well what you do is up to you and if you want to do things you will have to make time to do them. You will also have to be realistic. There is no point putting something like "Go on a Cruise" on your list as drawing that one out is just going to upset you unless you have that sort of money laying around!

Exercise

This is the time to make a list of all those things you would like to do. You will have to make your list realistic and things that you can do with little or no cost at all. What you are spending is your time and what you will get back is far more valuable. You may have to trade time you would spend doing something else but you can always do that "something else" another day if it is something you do regularly.

If you make it simple achievable things like "Take a Walk", "Read a Book", "Watch a Film", "Listen to a Specific Song" (or random, see "Music Jar" later).

The list will be very personal to you and things that you will enjoy.

You are doing them for you. You can talk about them to others but while you are doing them you are doing them for you and you must do them alone.

As you think of something you want to do, write it down here and later you can put it in your jar.

Once your jar has suggestions in it and you have some time and you want to do something you can pull out a suggestion. If you would like something specific which is already in your jar you can take that piece of paper out. If you complete the "thing" then you can put that in another jar, your "Completed Jar", if not it goes back into the "Jar List" to try again or to do again.

If you specifically enjoy doing something and you have done it then put it in another jar which is "Things you Enjoy" and you can revisit it and do it again at any time. If you have some spare time, choose a jar and then either do something random or pick out a few things and choose one to do.

It should save you spending your spare time wondering what to do!

CLEAR THE MIND

The mind is a wonderful thing and it can come up with some wonderful ideas, especially when you aren't in a position to remember them!

Also, ideas in the mind clutter the mind and can be a stress in themselves. If you want to get them out of your mind without losing them then write them down here! I started keeping a notebook beside my bed as I knew I'd have an idea in the night and by the morning this wonderful idea would be mist on the wind if it wasn't written down quickly.

Carrying a small notebook and pencil or pen with you at all times can be both amusing and rewarding. Perhaps you could carry this book with you? People have kept journals for years, they are invaluable for downloading all that information and thoughts that otherwise will clutter your hard drive (brain!). The ideas are still there, you can revisit them at any time and take them further.

The more you work your mind, the more it works. It needs to fire up and think and "be" and if you don't allow it to exercise itself it will find other ways to amuse itself, usually in the form of anxiety and depression as then it has your attention.

It may be that you feel that your job is "mundane" and your time wasted. On the contrary, you are in the very beneficial situation of having time to think and imagine other things. Your mind is free as in doing something repetitive you don't need to really be there all the time as long as you concentrate enough to "get it right" and do your best.

As part of my job in the past I had to sort out the law books. Their pages came in regularly as things changed and the pages had to be changed. I volunteered to do that which amazed the Partners and my colleagues as it was something very mundane. The Receptionist who usually did it was very busy, I had some spare time so I didn't mind and my philosophy has always been "Ours is not to do or die, ours is just to pacify". So if the books weren't up to date there would be stress, I didn't want the stress so I was happy to do the "menial task". That was until I realized that during that repetitive time of taking one page out and replacing it with another page with the same number from the new sheets I had time to think. It was a time when the body was busy and the mind could think through what it wanted to free of any need or responsibility to do anything else. Truly "my time".

This became mucking out time when I got the smallholding. I truly love mucking out as you start with a pile of poo and little by little it can be shovelled into the wheelbarrow and wheeled somewhere else. The big task is done and the mundane actions leave so much time to think which is truly personal time.

That is if you do it alone. If you do it with others of course it is a lovely social time where you can chatter about anything you like as you don't have to concentrate. So it was a little upsetting when we upgraded the barn in size and had to use a bobcat, that was just a mechanical exercise and other than driving the machine no fun at all!

Any time you have something to do that is repetitive and you don't need to concentrate on it then you have time for you.

It could be time to have this book with you to make those notes as you have no idea what ideas will come up and you don't want to lose them! Save them for later when you read them back and perhaps they will be the seed of something great.

There are always things in your life you should focus on but sometimes there just isn't time.

The worry is there that you should, something happens and then they are gone, into the ether, but not from your sub-conscious. They will be there, nibbling away as those little "niggles" of what you should be doing.

Exercise

Don't let them bother you. If you get a thought of something you should focus on and do then either write it down here or write it on a bit of paper, put it in a jar and when you get some time, draw a "Focus" from the jar and do it! Then throw the bit of paper away into the recycling. Or you can put it in another jar marked "Jobs done" (see later).

By working through your problems you will see the jar empty slowly. It may fill up again as you add to it but bit by bit you will get there and most importantly you can physically see what you need to deal with so they don't need to float around your mind bothering you.

What these are will be personal to you. As you do one job there will be other bits that need doing. Perhaps you won't finish a job and you have a tiny bit to do to make it complete? Perhaps you need to call someone who you haven't called for a while? It doesn't have to be a dramatic big thing, it is still something that will "niggle".

Put your niggles in a jar, take them out, deal with them and they will soon be gone!

POP IT IN A JAR

I discovered poppets a while back. I prefer to call them Care Dolls. They are a simple doll shaped object which can be decorated with an intent. I'd extend this to them being a doll which you can put in a jar, especially if they are cut them from cardboard as they will last and you can add beads, brooches or other things which you don't necessarily need to wear but would like to keep.

As long as you have the basic shape and you end up with something which looks like a doll you can use any medium you like. There are plenty of templates on the internet or you could draw your own. Perhaps you could cut from cardboard and then paint and decorate or perhaps felt, hand sew it and fill it with cotton wool or shredded non-recyclable plastic. It is up to you how creative you want to be.

When your doll is made he or she will need eyes and a mouth. Perhaps you will clothe your doll, perhaps you'll decorate it as it is.

These dolls are a great way to use broken bits and pieces of jewellery, odd beads, odd buttons, bits of wool, and other bits and pieces you may have around.

You can also tie sticks together to make a doll.

It is the intent that is important. As you are making it focus on what you want the doll to be. If you want him or her for luck, think about being lucky etc.

When you have finished your doll put him or her in the jar and put things in the jar which relate to what you want the doll to bring you. If love perhaps hearts cut from red paper or plastic that you find. If luck then perhaps cut clovers and horseshoes from paper or plastic you have around. If marriage then if you go to a wedding pick up some of the confetti from the ground, bless the couple and take a little of that happiness home with you and put it in with your doll.

The possibilities are endless and everything you use can be totally free.

You don't need expensive materials to make something amazing.

FOCUS JAR

NEGATIVE AND POSITIVE

Negative thoughts sneak around in the darkness, they wake you up, they poke you when you least want to be poked. But, they have no power over you other than be annoying and sometimes they are there for a reason.

Here you need two jars and both of them are for Negative Thoughts.

When you have a negative thought write it down. Then look at it. Is there a reason why you have had that thought? Is it a reminder to do something? Is it a hint that something you are doing needs a bit of looking at and thinking through? Or does it belong in the other category of a negative thought that has no solution and is just a "niggle".

Exercise

Take that piece of paper to cut up and your two jars. One is for Positive Negative Thoughts, the other is for Totally Pointless Negative Thoughts. Or you can write them here.

There are plenty of chemicals which run around in your system from food, drink, the environment and other sources which cause mischief for your emotions. They can cause emotions and those emotions are nothing to do with you. Knowing the difference helps!

The thought will be in front of you in black and white. It is your decision whether it is for you, or pointless annoyance. You will have to be honest though as it is your decision and this is totally personal to you which jar you put it in. Nobody can tell you why you are having that thought but if there is no reason for it, put it in the Pointless Jar and put the lid on it. It can't hurt you then.

If it is for the Positive Negative Jar (which negates the emotion as a positive and a negative will cancel themselves out) then you have a reminder. Why is it there? Is there something you should do? Is there a question in your mind which needs answering? Is there a "real doubt" which you need to answer?

If it is an answer that is needed this can be as simple as "Yes, I'm right it is ok" then you can throw the thought into the Pointless Pot. If it is not then why have you thought it? Do you need to sort something out so it goes away as it has done its job. Knowing the difference makes that worry a very valuable asset rather than a depressive pointless darkness in a happy day.

GRATEFULLY ADJAR

I nearly forgot to say thank you... I think those are the lyrics in a song I heard years ago but we often forget to be grateful for the good things that happen in our life. The kindness of strangers and the lovely things that people do.

Years ago I was rushing around in my lunch hour trying to get far too many things done. It was raining and I'd left my umbrella at home. Days earlier a company had been handing out umbrellas as an advertising stunt. I was soaked and it was then when a complete stranger stopped me. He was just going down into the underground and he said that he no longer needed his free umbrella and I was welcome to it. It was a simple good deed, it did stop me having an afternoon of being very wet at work but it was a kindness which I have never forgotten.

There are lots of things like that every day that we forget to notice. It is easy to remember when someone does something nasty but how about all those times when someone does something nice. These are nice things that cost nothing but should mean the world but we forget to notice them.

Exercise

When you get the time and something has happened then write them down here. Put them on a piece of paper and put them in your Grateful Jar. You may never take them out and read them again but you can look at the jar and see those pieces of paper growing and know that there is good in the world.

Why not have another jar for good things that you have done? Be grateful to yourself for doing these things and make a record of them. Again, you may never go back and read them but if you ever doubt yourself, look at them and that is the good you have done.

Who knows when doing a simple deed of goodwill that it can become something quite magnificent. You will of course never know as the person goes on into the world and you may never see them again but the influence of that good deed could make them do something that has a great resonance in the world. Or you made someone happy, even if it is only for a moment.

One moment is better than a lifetime without.

NOTE POUCH

You can't take a jar with you and you may not be able to take this book with you all the time so you could make yourself a note pouch. They are small pouches which can keep your pieces of paper together until you get home and can put them in their right jars.

TINY JARS

It is also possible to buy tiny jars or you may have a small jar from something you bought to use. These are for single memories or things which are important to you, small finds and things you want to keep and remember. Having them on a shelf where you can see them and remember helps to bring back happy times or remember someone or something important.

BE JAR

We all have people we want to be and sometimes we don't quite measure up to how we would like to be.

Exercise

A good way to start is to write on slips of paper or here all the things you would like to "be".

You aren't immediately going to become that person but you can make a start by writing them down. Then when you actually become like that or do something along those lines take the slip of paper out and mark a little line on it. For the fifth one cross it across. You will watch yourself becoming more the person you want to be, bit by bit.

Perhaps it is something like:

Open Minded

Eager to Explore New Avenues

Able to Recognise Opportunities

Able to See the Other Person's Point of View

Able to Seize the Moment

Able to try new Paths

Able to take time to think

The choices are yours to write. They are simple things, not life changing in themselves but things you would like to see in yourself.

Perhaps you are seeing them in others. It doesn't help to write them down and put them in the jar. You never know, once in a while you might see it in yourself.

MOODY JAR

Sometimes we have Moods which are not our own. Having a Mood Jar might help.

Exercise

If you have a mood that you can feel then if it isn't already in the jar take a piece of paper and write it down. Then sit and think about the piece of paper. Is there a reason why you feel like that?

Has something happened which has caused this mood? If so, what can you do to make things change or is it something you just have to live though?

If it is a realistic mood then put a little tick on the piece of paper, put it back in the jar and accept that very soon the situation will change and you will feel better.

If you have a mood and you can't find any real reason for it then it is one of those "emotions that aren't yours". Put a cross on the piece of paper, put it back in the jar and go to another jar with a "task" and take one out and focus on that.

Or, if it is a mood you can't associate with anything you feel, take a pen and write a story which reflects that mood and use the energy. Put it aside and collect them up. One day you may have a novel of short stories! Use the emotion and you take its power away, you turn something negative into something positive and then it can no longer harm you as it is nothing to do with you.

If you aren't creative then take a piece of junk mail and cut out a bit of the colour that you associate with that mood and put it in a tiny jar. As the colours build up you will have a pretty jar. Don't forget to put the happy moods in there too and you'll have something that is amusing to look at.

MUSIC JAR

If you feel that you need support without there being the need to tell others or share it with others then it may help to find music which suits your mood and the situation. It can be the lyrics or the tune. It can be the music that suits your mood or completely opposite, the music which will get you out of your mood.

Exercise

If you can't listen to the music at the time as you are at work etc then write it here or on a piece of paper and put it in your Music Jar when you get home and listen to it when you can.

When you get the time to play the music then you can let the thoughts wash over you and that music is in your memory for when you need it. The thoughts can float away in the air, like the music.

Music should be enjoyed but it can also be great for changing your mood or reflecting it. For this it is probably better to organize a playlist or just play music as you feel like you need to hear it.

If you prefer something more random then a jar comes in handy for this too. A song on each piece of paper in the jar can be a great way to pick out a song which can be very relevant or just something you want to listen to.

If you specifically enjoy music and it really helps you with your moods and making decisions etc then why not have a jar for each type of music and then put pieces of paper with songs written on them in the jar which corresponds with one of your moods. .

PROBLEM JAR

If you look at what you have to do and solve sometimes it seems like an impossible situation. It isn't, in time you'll sort it out but you need the clarity to make a start.

The Problem Jar can help with that as it breaks your problems down into small chunks.

Exercise

This requires two jars. The "jobs to be done" jar and the "jobs done" jar.

Write down all the jobs you have to do, all the tasks and all the phone calls and everything else. You can write them here and cross them off or on a piece of paper and cut them up.

Take a pair of scissors and cut the page up if you choose the separate page method, cutting each item off separately. Then fold them up and put them in the jar.

If things are urgent then put a cross on the folded piece of paper, if not, leave it blank.

When you have time to do something then pull out a piece of paper and do that thing.

If some of those jobs require other things to go with them then make that list on the paper when you make the original note of the problem. Then you can easily gather what you need, get the job done and once done you can put that bit of paper in another jar marked "done".

As one jar lessens and the other fills hopefully you will have a great feeling of satisfaction. You can physically see what you have done.

Some jobs are repetitive and you don't see any real reward for doing them. Of course you see the results when you don't do them! Getting them done one by one is a good step along the way to getting on top of your problems, that will make you feel better and more able to deal with the problems and things you have to do as they arise in the future.

JARRING PEOPLE

There are always people who are going to annoy you. If asking them politely to stop doesn't work then you are going to have to cope with the situation. You have two choices, react quickly and give them what they want while being controlled about it and knowing it is your choice or don't react at all and let them know that you know what they are doing.

If you can find your "Serenity", your calm space, then nobody can "get to you". It does take time to get to that spot as it is so easy to answer back, to feel inadequate, to feel that you are the one in the wrong.

Look at any situation, if you are at fault, admit it. Of course you have to admit it to yourself first. Once you are assured in your own belief then you can work out if the other person's comments are justified. If they are then apologise and do what you can to put things right. If they then find something else, then you have your answer. They actually want to cause trouble. If not then they were justified.

There is a big difference between arrogance and confidence. Confidence is a good place where you know what you are doing and why you are doing it. Arrogance is doing something just to be "in charge" or because you have to be right.

Everyone has views and they have thoughts and a life too. They have reasons why they do or say what they do. If you know why they are doing it then you can deal with it.

It was explained to me as being like someone offering you a biscuit. They offer the biscuit with all that it means. If you accept the biscuit then you experience it. If you don't take the biscuit it stays with them.

It is hard and it can make you feel awful but don't let them win. Once you know it is "their game" you can win yourself just by making the situation go the way you want it to. If they need to feel self-gratification by putting you down, that is the only way they can be happy then sometimes let them feel like they have won. The "silent victory" can be just as satisfying.

However, that could be a time to re-evaluate whether that is the relationship or friendship you should be in. Walking away isn't always that easy and in other ways they may be fine.

Again an "Emotion Jar" may help. If you write down every incident and put it in the jar, or here, then you have all the times you were upset if you ever want to check back and feel more assured that you are right in your thinking. It may be that by nature you are forgiving, sometimes there is a situation where you have to stop forgiving and do what is right for someone else as well.

Alternatively it may be that the "someone" has their own issues and they are "just like that". Then it is your choice whether you accept it and deal with it and manage it in the best way that you can accepting that nobody is perfect.

The textbook Prince Charming does not exist.

Knowing there is a problem is the first step to putting it right. It can be a partner, a neighbour, a friend, someone you know. It doesn't matter, write their name, write what they have done and put it in the jar. Later when you have a moment take the piece of paper out and write how you feel about it. Put it back in the jar and later take it out again and write what you can do about it.

Most importantly tell people about it. Don't keep it to yourself.

Sometimes it can be that there isn't anything else to focus on. The more you have in your life, the less important it is. If you are sitting around all day worrying about someone who is causing you emotional harm then they are winning. They really aren't that important and it is only you who is making them important. If you can't ignore them then at least make sure that whatever they do is impotent. You are a strong being who is sensitive and you wouldn't be worried if you didn't care. Being able to care is a wonderful part of you, don't let it be a weapon to be used against you.

If you can't ignore them then internally laugh at them and play your role to get the minimum amount of difficulty. If they need to belittle someone and they aren't too close to you e.g. a person you know then it could be their empowerment to belittle others. Just smile, walk away and if you can't help them, let them go out of your life.

If you work with them then just get on with what you have to do and make them as unimportant to you as you can. They have the problem, not you and don't let their problem become yours.

HAVING A FOCUS

IF YOU ARE HAVING PROBLEMS WITH FOCUSING THEN EITHER CHOOSE ONE OF YOUR OWN NECKLACES OR BUY SOMETHING NEW AND USE IT AS A FOCUS. SIT QUIETLY WITH IT, HOLDING IT AND THINK OR SAY OVER AND OVER AGAIN "THIS IS MY SAFE PLACE" WHILE FOCUSING ON BEING CALM. THINK IT, SAY IT AND THEN WHEN SOMEONE ANNOYS YOU, TOUCH THE NECKLACE AND LET THE CALM WASH OVER YOU.

Printed in Great Britain
by Amazon